THE CHANGING YEARS
MY RELATIONSHIPS WITH OTHERS

by
Mary Anne McElmurry, O.P., M.A.
Judith Bisignano, O.P., Ed. D.

illustrated by
Kay Mirocha

Cover by Kathryn Hyndman
Copyright © Good Apple, Inc., 1987

GOOD APPLE, INC.
299 JEFFERSON ROAD
P.O. BOX 480
PARSIPPANY, NJ 07054-0480

All rights reserved. Printed in the United States of America.

Copyright © Good Apple, Inc., 1987
ISBN No. 0-86653-419-9
Printing No. 98765432

The purchase of this book entitles the buyer to duplicate the student activity pages for classroom use only. Any other use requires written permission from Good Apple, Inc.

GOOD APPLE, INC.
299 JEFFERSON ROAD
P.O. BOX 480
PARSIPPANY, NJ 07054-0480

All rights reserved. Printed in the United States of America.

Description of Kino Learning Center

Kino Learning Center is a private, nonprofit elementary and secondary school founded in Tucson, Arizona, in 1975 by parents seeking an alternative learning environment for children. The school is staffed by 20 teachers and has an enrollment of 200 students between the ages of 3 and 18.

At Kino Learning Center the students, teachers, and parents form a learning community in which people are bound together in mutual aid, responsibility and cooperation. Freedom exists within this interaction as the liberty persons grant to each other out of their faith in and concern for one another. Such freedom is nourished by mutual respect and appreciation; from it, trust grows and individuality flourishes.

Within the prepared learning environment of the school, each child is free to choose from worthwhile options, a sequence of activities unique to his/her needs and experiences, and in which he/she finds success, interest, and pleasure. Each child is free to develop in the way and at the pace appropriate to his/her needs, abilities, and interests. The school places special stress on individual discovery, on firsthand experience, and on creative work.

At Kino Learning Center, adults and children mutually engaged in the learning process are continually in the process of changing and growing, for to learn is to change. And to experience joy in learning is to delight in life itself, for learning and life are one.

TABLE OF CONTENTS

	Page
I. UNDERSTANDING MYSELF	1
Recognizing Personality Traits	1
Extrovert or Introvert	3
Intuitive or Sensate	6
Thinker or Feeler	9
Judger or Perceiver	12
II. IMPROVING PEER RELATIONS	15
Guidelines for Quality Friendships	15
Knowing Myself	22
Dealing with Peer Pressure	24
Determining My Values	25
Working Things Out	27
III. IMPROVING FAMILY RELATIONS	31
Rules Around the House	31
Stating Expectations	33
Finding Privacy	35
Discussing Problems	37
Showing Appreciation	41
Growing as a Family	42
IV. IMPROVING ADULT RELATIONS	43
Adult Influences	43
Relating to My Parents	44
Relating to Older People	45
Relating to Teachers	47
Relating to Employers	48
Relating to Employees	49
Relating to Doctors	50
Influence of Media	51
Evaluation	54
Bibliography	57

INTRODUCTION

A message to students.

The road to adulthood is not without obstacles. You will take risks that will strengthen and shake your self-confidence. You will make decisions that will demonstrate both good and poor judgment. You will invest in relationships that will be both short-lived and long lasting. Some people will expect you to act older than you feel. Others will treat you like a child when you feel quite mature. All this can be quite confusing.

My Relationships with Others is a workbook intended to assist you in your transition from adolescence to adulthood. The activities are designed to help you better understand yourself, as well as improve your relations with your family, friends and adults who influence your life.

One important aspect of *My Relationships with Others* is the opportunity to discuss your ideas, attitudes and opinions with your friends and classmates. The choice for discussion is clearly marked with this symbol:

This book is intended to help you view your road to adulthood as one that is paved with opportunities rather than obstacles. Your pace and direction is a personal choice. May your travels result in much happiness today and all the days ahead.

A message to teachers.

As adults, we most likely remember our adolescent years as a very stressful and threatening time in our lives. We recall the "mysterious" physical changes that occurred during those early years. We remember the feelings of self-doubt and inferiority that seemed unbearable at times. We recall our emotional vulnerability to failure and our fear of rejection from peers and parents. As adults, we typically keep these memories to ourselves. Our silence causes today's teenagers to experience the same and greater disorientation that we experienced during our adolescent years.

Adolescence is distressing because young people do not fully understand the physical, psychological and social changes taking place in their lives. Many fears and anxieties could be eliminated by simple explanations presented in a personal, encouraging manner by parents and teachers.

This book is one of a four-book series written specifically for boys and girls between the ages of eleven and fourteen. It is written in words and terms that can be easily understood by the reader. The book is intended to help teenagers better understand themselves as well as to better understand and appreciate others.

As a concerned adult and important role model, you will want to preview this book prior to use by your students. It is also important to let parents review this material since they have the primary responsibility for the growth and development of their children.

Parents will most likely appreciate your personal and professional interest in the total growth of their child. When parents and teachers work together, the knowledge, attitudes and values imparted will be useful tools for children as they, too, make the transition from adolescence to adulthood.

I. UNDERSTANDING MYSELF

You must know and care about yourself before you can understand and appreciate others. Your responses to the following activities will help you identify the unique qualities and characteristics of yourself and others.

• RECOGNIZING PERSONALITY TRAITS

Take the time to observe the personality traits of the various people in your class. Write the name of a classmate described in each of the statements below. You may repeat the name of a particular person if necessary. You may write more than one name for a statement if necessary. REMEMBER, NO PERSONALITY TRAIT IS BETTER THAN ANOTHER.

1. _____ enjoys being with other people.
2. _____ enjoys being alone.
3. _____ is quick to meet new people.
4. _____ is cautious about meeting new people.
5. _____ always seems to know what is happening.
6. _____ tends to have missed the latest news.
7. _____ trusts his/her feelings.
8. _____ trusts his/her information and experiences.

9. _____ likes variety.
10. _____ likes routine.
11. _____ enjoys thinking about ideas.
12. _____ enjoys talking with people.
13. _____ tends to hold in his/her feelings.
14. _____ tends to openly share his/her feelings.
15. _____ tends to be forceful with other people.
16. _____ tends to be gentle with other people.
17. _____ likes planned activities.
18. _____ likes spontaneous activities.
19. _____ makes decisions quickly.
20. _____ gets all the information before making a decision.
21. _____ tends to be serious.
22. _____ tends to be easygoing.
23. _____ deals with facts.
24. _____ deals with people.
25. _____ _____
26. _____ _____
27. _____ _____
28. _____ _____
29. _____ _____
30. _____ _____

• EXTROVERT OR INTROVERT

The following statements will help you determine if you are a person who is an *introvert* or an *extrovert*. Check (√) the statement that best describes how you usually feel or act.

1. When I relax I usually like to

    _____ a. be with people.
    _____ b. be alone.

2. At a party, I usually feel

    _____ a. comfortable.
    _____ b. out of place.

3. I am

    _____ a. easy to get to know.
    _____ b. cautious about meeting new people.

4. At parties I usually

    _____ a. like to stay until the end.
    _____ b. leave after a short period of time.

5. On my lunch break I usually

    _____ a. visit with friends.
    _____ b. sit in a comfortable place by myself.

6. I prefer to have

    _____ a. many friends.
    _____ b. a few close friends.

7. Spontaneous get-togethers with friends

   _____ a. are enjoyable.
   _____ b. are annoying.

8. In a group I usually

   _____ a. begin the conversation.
   _____ b. wait for someone else to talk first.

9. When I am with my friends I usually

   _____ a. know what is going on.
   _____ b. get behind on the latest news.

10. When I am by myself I usually

    _____ a. miss having people around.
    _____ b. enjoy the time alone.

Record your answers to the above statements on the chart below. Record the total number of checks for answers *a* and answers *b*.

QUESTION NUMBER	ANSWER a	b
1		
2		
3		
4		
5		
6		
7		
8		
9		
10		
Total		

The *a* answers describe a person who is an *extrovert*.
The *b* answers describe a person who is an *introvert*.

SUMMARY:

A person who is an *extrovert*:

- enjoys talking, working and playing with people.
- enjoys parties and events where there are many people.
- finds it easy to start and continue conversations.
- enjoys a variety of daily activities.
- sometimes acts before thinking.

A person who is an *introvert*:

- enjoys being alone.
- enjoys being with people, but finds it draining of energy to do so.
- finds it difficult to communicate with people.
- enjoys working alone.
- thinks before acting.
- enjoys working on one thing for an extended time.

Discuss with your classmates those characteristics of an extrovert and introvert which you possess.

Circle one:

I would generally describe myself as

    an extrovert.

    an introvert.

• INTUITIVE OR SENSATE

The following statements will help you determine if you are a person who is *intuitive* or *sensate*. Check (√) the statement that best describes how you usually feel or act.

1. I like people who are

    _____ a. sensible and down to earth.
    _____ b. imaginative and unpredictable.

2. I am a person who

    _____ a. wants facts before taking action.
    _____ b. follows a dream.

3. In books and magazines, I most enjoy

    _____ a. the written words.
    _____ b. the pictures.

4. I trust

    _____ a. my facts.
    _____ b. my feelings.

5. I like

    _____ a. doing things I know how to do.
    _____ b. doing new things.

6. I like

    _____ a. routine in my life.
    _____ b. variety in my life.

7. I am a person who

    _____ a. wants things well-planned with no surprises.
    _____ b. does not mind last minute changes.

8. I tend to see

    _____ a. things to be done now.
    _____ b. things to be done in the future.

6

9. I like to

_____ a. work with well thought out ideas.
_____ b. work with new ideas.

10. I like to know

_____ a. what others are thinking.
_____ b. what others are doing.

Record your answers to the above statements on the chart below. Record the total number of checks for answers *a* and answers *b*.

QUESTION NUMBER	ANSWER a	b
1		
2		
3		
4		
5		
6		
7		
8		
9		
10		
Total		

The *a* answers describe a person who is sensate.
The *b* answers describe a person who is intuitive.

7

SUMMARY:

A person who is *sensate*:

- enjoys routine.
- solves a problem one step at a time.
- is usually correct about facts.
- is more interested in the past than the future.
- notices details.
- tolerates little nonsense when getting a job completed.

A person who is *intuitive*:

- enjoys daydreaming.
- is more concerned about the future than the past.
- likes to talk about possibilities.
- likes to improve a situation.
- enjoys thinking about what is ideal rather than what is real.
- starts a new job without completing an old job.

Discuss with your classmates those sensate or intuitive characteristics which you possess.

Circle one:

I would generally describe myself as

sensate.

intuitive.

• THINKER OR FEELER

The following statements will help you determine if you are a *thinking* person or a *feeling* person. Check (√) the statement that best describes you.

1. I usually enjoy

    _____ a. thinking about ideas.
    _____ b. talking with people.

2. When making decisions, I am most concerned about

    _____ a. the rules and regulations related to a decision.
    _____ b. how people will be affected by the decision.

3. When dealing with people, I am more concerned with

    _____ a. being fair.
    _____ b. being friendly.

4. When dealing with a problem, I am more concerned with

    _____ a. the facts involved.
    _____ b. the people involved.

5. I sometimes find myself

    _____ a. hurting people's feelings.
    _____ b. trying too hard to please people.

6. Concerning my feelings, I usually

    _____ a. keep them private.
    _____ b. share them openly.

7. I usually consider myself to be

    _____ a. a hard-headed person.
    _____ b. a soft-hearted person.

8. I usually act from

   _____ a. my head.
   _____ b. my heart.

9. When talking with others, I usually want to

   _____ a. deal with facts.
   _____ b. deal with people.

10. When relating to people, I am usually

    _____ a. firm.
    _____ b. gentle.

Record your answers to the above statements on the chart below. Record the total number of checks for answers *a* and answers *b*.

QUESTION NUMBER	ANSWER a	b
1		
2		
3		
4		
5		
6		
7		
8		
9		
10		
Total		

The *a* answers describe a thinking person.
The *b* answers describe a feeling person.

10

SUMMARY:

A *thinking* person:

- does not show feelings easily.
- may hurt others' feelings without realizing it.
- enjoys reasoning about a situation.
- listens to facts rather than feelings.
- may tend to appear cold and distant.
- tries to be fair at all times.

A *feeling* person:

- shows feelings openly.
- may tend to be moody.
- desires peace and harmony in relationships.
- is very sympathetic.
- is someone in whom others can confide.
- often needs to be patted on the back.

Discuss with your classmates those characteristics of a thinking and feeling person which you possess.

Circle one:

I would generally describe myself as

a thinking person.

a feeling person.

• JUDGER OR PERCEIVER

The following statements will help you determine if you are a *judging* person or a *perceiving* person. Check (√) the statement that best describes how you usually feel and act.

1. When I am working on a project, I usually prefer

    _____ a. an established deadline.
    _____ b. my own time line.

2. I usually like

    _____ a. planned activities.
    _____ b. spontaneous activities.

3. I feel more challenged

    _____ a. after I have made a decision.
    _____ b. before I have made a decision.

4. I usually like

    _____ a. things in a settled state.
    _____ b. things in the working stage.

5. I am usually someone who

    _____ a. has to get things completed.
    _____ b. can work on things forever.

6. I usually like days that are

    _____ a. scheduled.
    _____ b. spontaneous.

7. I usually like

    _____ a. to make quick decisions.
    _____ b. to postpone decisions until I reconsider all the facts.

12

8. I usually like

   _____ a. to know exactly what is expected of me.
   _____ b. the freedom to do what I want.

9. I tend to be

   _____ a. serious.
   _____ b. easygoing.

10. When making a decision, I usually

    _____ a. plan carefully.
    _____ b. decide quickly.

Record your answers to the above statements on the chart below. Record the total number of checks for answers *a* and answers *b*.

QUESTION NUMBER	ANSWER a	b
1		
2		
3		
4		
5		
6		
7		
8		
9		
10		
Total		

The *a* answers describe a *judgmental* person.
The *b* answers describe a *perceptive* person.

13

SUMMARY:

A *judgmental* person:

- gets things done.
- likes to be on time.
- likes planned activities.
- likes to make decisions quickly.
- may tend to be stubborn.
- may tend to overlook some options when making a decision.

A *perceptive* person:

- is spontaneous.
- has trouble making decisions.
- likes changes and interruptions to one's routine.
- tends to get things done at the last minute.
- may tend to stand back and watch things happen.
- enjoys many things going on at the same time.

Discuss with your classmates those characteristics of a judgmental and a perceptive person.

Circle one:

I would generally describe myself as

a judgmental person.

a perceptive person.

14

II. IMPROVING PEER RELATIONS

Acquiring and maintaining quality relationships is an important part of adolescence. Lasting friendships require consistent effort on the part of all participants.

GUIDELINES FOR QUALITY FRIENDSHIPS

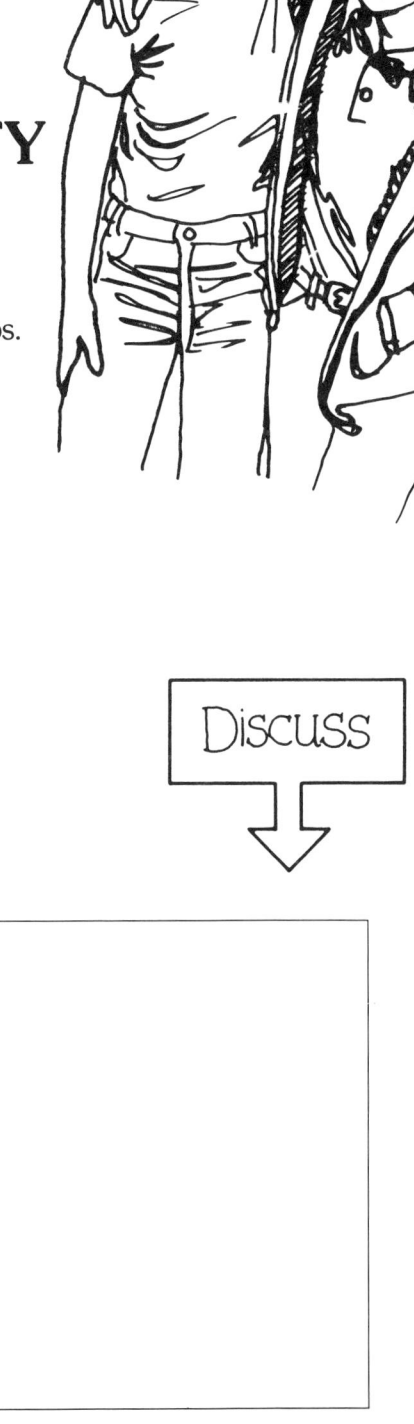

Listed below are guidelines for developing quality friendships. Add your own guidelines for developing and maintaining good relationships.

1. Recognize one another's likes and dislikes.
2. Recognize one another's needs.
3. Accept one another's uniquenesses.
4. Keep relations free of expectations.
5. Take responsibility for honest communication.
6. Allow one another the freedom to develop other quality friendships.

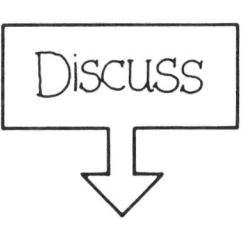

15

RECOGNIZING ONE ANOTHER'S LIKES AND DISLIKES

It is important to analyze your likes and dislikes in order to determine what you have in common with other people. Circle your response to each statement according to the following scale.

1. always
2. often
3. sometimes
4. seldom
5. never

I like to

a. stay up late and watch television.   1 2 3 4 5

b. sleep late on Saturdays.   1 2 3 4 5

c. be on time for appointments.   1 2 3 4 5

d. talk on the phone.   1 2 3 4 5

e. read for pleasure.   1 2 3 4 5

f. go to the movies.   1 2 3 4 5

g. relax around the house.   1 2 3 4 5

h. eat at restaurants.   1 2 3 4 5

i. listen to music.   1 2 3 4 5

j. keep my bedroom organized.   1 2 3 4 5

k. buy my own clothes.   1 2 3 4 5

l. earn my own money.   1 2 3 4 5

m. exercise my body.   1 2 3 4 5

n. give of my time and talents.   1 2 3 4 5

o. be successful.   1 2 3 4 5

p. have close friendships.   1 2 3 4 5

q. spend time on my appearance.   1 2 3 4 5

r. _____   1 2 3 4 5

s. _____   1 2 3 4 5

t. _____   1 2 3 4 5

• RECOGNIZING ONE ANOTHER'S NEEDS

Complete the bar graph to indicate the degree to which you need each of the following.

	LOW	MODERATE	HIGH
ATTENTION			
UNDERSTANDING			
RECOGNITION			
ENCOURAGEMENT			
AFFECTION			

Complete the bar graph to indicate the degree to which you usually offer each of the following to your friends.

	LOW	MODERATE	HIGH
ATTENTION			
UNDERSTANDING			
RECOGNITION			
ENCOURAGEMENT			
AFFECTION			

• ACCEPTING ONE ANOTHER'S UNIQUENESSES

Teenagers often like to fit in with their friends. Being able to accept (and even appreciate) those things that make you stand out may bring you great comfort in a crowd. Complete the sentences below.

If I were to describe myself using three positive words, I would say that I am

_____

_____

_____

One of the most unique things about me is

_____

_____

_____

One of the most unique things that ever happened to me was

_____

_____

_____

A unique goal I hope to accomplish in the future is

_____

_____

_____

Share your uniqueness by discussing your responses with your classmates.

Discuss

• KEEPING RELATIONS FREE OF UNSPOKEN EXPECTATIONS

It is very difficult (if not impossible) for a friend to know and fulfill your secret expectations. Discuss your thoughts and feelings regarding unspoken expectations in a friendship.

Tell about an unspoken expectation you often have of your friends. Describe your feelings when these expectations are not met.

Tell about your feelings when friends have unspoken expectations of you. Discuss with your friends how expectations might be either articulated or eliminated.

Share your suggestions for keeping relations free of unspoken expectations in the space below.

_____
_____
_____
_____
_____
_____
_____
_____

• COMMUNICATING HONESTLY

Honest communication is essential for maintaining quality relationships. Check (✓) the degree to which you possess each of the following communication skills.

DISCUSS ⬇

	Usually	Sometimes	Seldom
1. I retain eye contact throughout the conversation.			
2. I keep an open mind throughout the conversation.			
3. I keep to the subject of the conversation.			
4. I ask the speaker to clarify aspects of the conversation that I do not understand.			
5. I visibly respond with facial and body gestures.			
6. I think about what is being said rather than what I am going to say.			

My greatest communication skill is
_____
_____
_____

One thing I could do to improve my communication skills is
_____
_____
_____

• ALLOWING FREEDOM IN FRIENDSHIPS

Quality friendships should expand rather than confine. Encouraging friends to develop other relationships is a true expression of unselfish affection. Such freedom generally results in stronger relationships between you and your friends.

Suggest an unselfish response to the situations below.

You are eating lunch with a friend. A stranger recognizes your friend and eagerly approaches the table.

Response: _____

You have planned a fun evening with a close friend who calls and tells you that an unexpected cousin has stopped in to visit.

Response: _____

Discuss with your classmates your responses to these situations.

• KNOWING MYSELF

It is important to evaluate your choice of friends and your motivation for choosing such friends.

Circle your response to each set of statements.

I have a close friend who is

a good student.	YES	NO
a poor student.	YES	NO
shy.	YES	NO
outgoing.	YES	NO
clumsy and awkward.	YES	NO
well-coordinated.	YES	NO
calm and relaxed.	YES	NO
easily excited.	YES	NO
popular with others.	YES	NO
unpopular with others.	YES	NO

Draw a general conclusion from your responses to the statements.

_____
_____
_____
_____
_____
_____

• KNOWING MYSELF

It is important to recognize the degree of contentment that you feel in your life as a teenager.

Check (✓) the appropriate response to each question.

	ALWAYS	USUALLY	SOMETIMES	SELDOM	NEVER
1. I feel powerless to do anything about my life.					
2. I have crying spells.					
3. It is easy for me to relax.					
4. I feel needed by others.					
5. I get upset easily.					
6. I have a great deal of fun.					
7. I enjoy being with other people.					
8. I feel that people really care about me.					

Discuss your answers and your degree of contentment with an adult whom you trust. Work out a plan for feeling more contented about your life. Put your plan into action.

My plan for greater contentment:

_____

_____

_____

_____

• DEALING WITH PEER PRESSURE

The need to be accepted by your friends is one of the strongest influences in your life as a teenager. It is important to recognize the degree of this influence in your life.

Check (✓) the degree of peer pressure you experience in the situations described below.

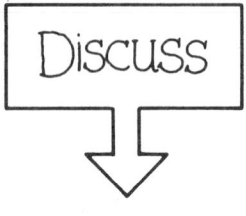

PRESSURE FROM MY PEERS	STRONGLY EXISTS	SOMEWHAT EXISTS	DOES NOT EXIST
1. to talk negatively about my parents			
2. to smoke			
3. to use alcohol and other drugs			
4. to use slang and swear words			
5. to like the opposite sex			
6. to have popular friends			
7. to be nice looking			
8. to dress in style			
9. to like popular songs and movies			
10. to dislike school			
11. to act cool			
12. _____			

Discuss with your classmates the pressures of coping with peer pressure. Discuss how you might go against peer pressure in a specific situation.

24

• DETERMINING MY VALUES

Your values are those beliefs and things that are important to you. You can counteract peer pressure by acting out of a clearly defined value system.

Check (✓) the degree to which you value each of the items below.

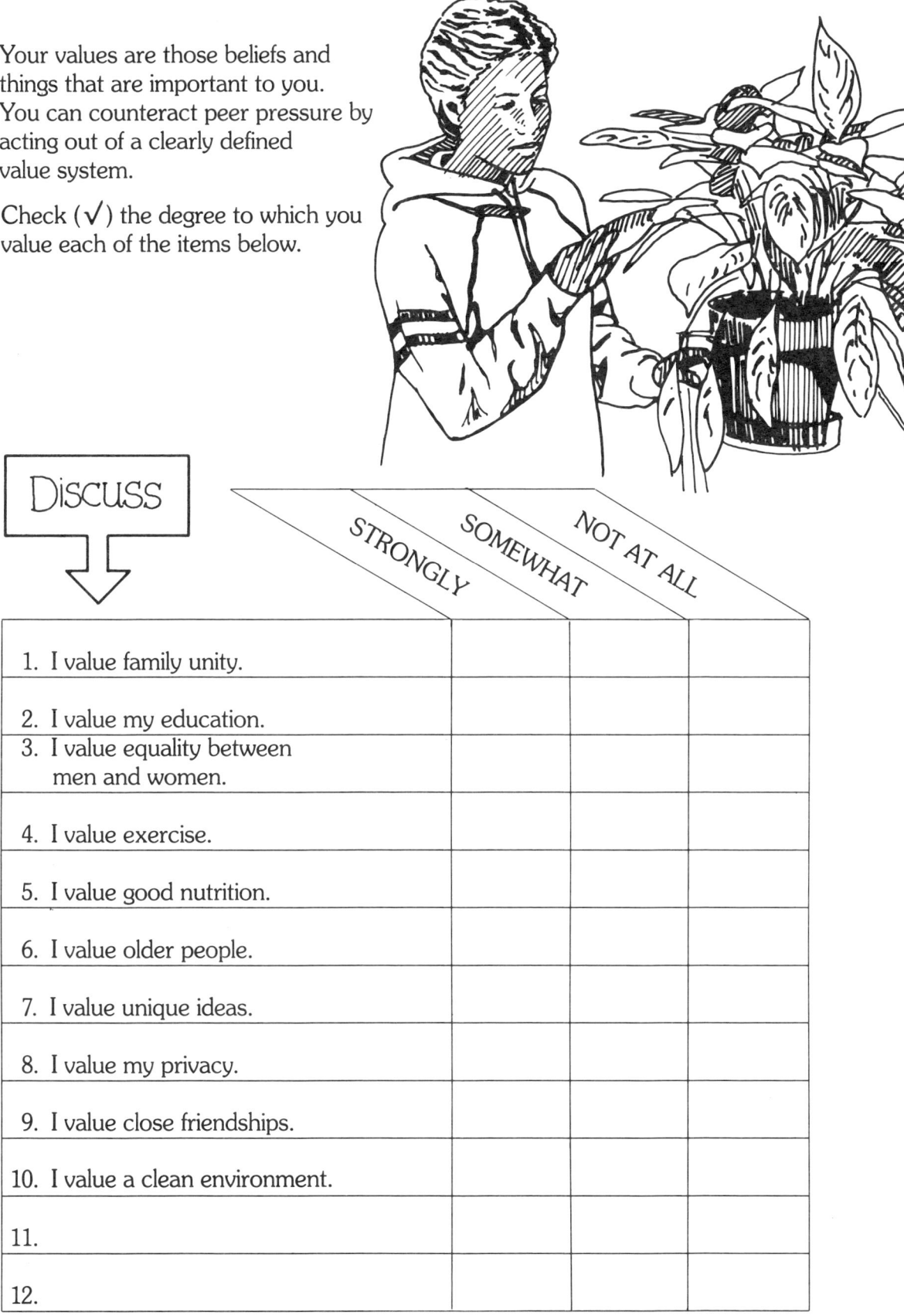

Discuss ⬇

	STRONGLY	SOMEWHAT	NOT AT ALL
1. I value family unity.			
2. I value my education.			
3. I value equality between men and women.			
4. I value exercise.			
5. I value good nutrition.			
6. I value older people.			
7. I value unique ideas.			
8. I value my privacy.			
9. I value close friendships.			
10. I value a clean environment.			
11.			
12.			

Discuss with your classmates those people and things you value most in life.

• ACTING INDEPENDENTLY

Peer pressure is the tension you experience when trying to be like your friends. It is important to feel confident enough to make choices independently of those made by your friends. Tell about those times you act independently of your friends.

Examples:

When leaving the house with my friends, I kiss my parents goodbye, even though my friends sometimes tease me about it.

I enjoy going to church even though some of my friends do not.

_____
_____
_____
_____
_____
_____
_____
_____
_____
_____
_____
_____
_____

Discuss with your classmates how you feel when acting independently of peer pressure.

• WORKING THINGS OUT

Described below are situations frequently experienced by teenagers. Discuss possible solutions to these common dilemmas.

Write your solution for each situation.

SITUATION:
You hear a false rumor about a good friend. If you try to stop the rumor, you risk becoming a part of it. What will you do?

SOLUTION: _____

_____

_____

SITUATION:
A good friend whom you really like asks you to go steady. You would like to go places with this person, but you would also like to be free to go with other people. If you refuse the offer, you may lose a good friend. What will you do?

SOLUTION: _____

_____

_____

SITUATION:
Several of your friends are smoking at the party. They offer you a cigarette. You don't want to smoke, but you don't want to be different. What will you do?

SOLUTION: _____

_____

_____

Describe a personal problem.

_____

_____

Ask a friend to suggest a solution to your situation.

_____

_____

• ACCEPTING OTHERS

If you generally accept other people and feel accepted by them, you are probably a happy person. A lack of acceptance by others can cause emptiness in your life.

Read the following statements. Check (✓) the appropriate response to determine your degree of acceptance of others.

	ALWAYS	USUALLY	SOMETIMES	SELDOM	NEVER
1. I like people I get to know.					
2. I am comfortable with nearly all kinds of people.					
3. With most people I know just where I stand.					
4. When you're nice to others, they will be nice in return.					
5. I enjoy going to parties.					
6. People are honest.					
7. People are pretty reasonable.					
8. You can get ahead without hurting people.					

Discuss the results of your survey with an adult whom you respect and admire. If you answered "sometimes," "seldom," or "never" to any statements, you may want to devise a plan whereby you become more accepting of other people. Put your plan into action.

My plan for greater acceptance:

_____

_____

_____

_____

SITUATION: You have a good friend with whom you constantly fight and argue. You believe that people who sincerely care about each other would not act this way. You do not want to discontinue the friendship but you do not want to continue the fighting. What will you do?

SOLUTION: _____

_____

_____

_____

_____

SITUATION: You have a friend with big feet, knobby knees and numerous pimples. His hair won't act like he wants it. He thinks he has all the charm of a week-old baloney sandwich. He is constantly putting himself down when he talks with you. What will you do?

SOLUTION: _____

_____

_____

_____

_____

SITUATION: You have a new friend and you feel like doing cartwheels across the campus. When the school band plays the victory song, it feels like they're playing it just for you. Something special is happening. It's hard to believe that one week ago you hardly knew this person. Your friend wants to get serious. What will you do?

SOLUTION: _____

_____

_____

_____

_____

• MEASURING PEER RELATIONS

Your peer group serves a very important function. This group provides you with guidelines for behavior, social contacts and a source for feeling good about yourself.

Check (✓) the appropriate response to measure the way you feel about the people with whom you work, play and associate.

	USUALLY	OFTEN	SOMETIMES	SELDOM	NEVER
1. I get along well with my peers.					
2. My peers care about me.					
3. My peers respect me.					
4. My peers understand me.					
5. I like my present peer group.					
6. I enjoy being with my peer group.					
7. My peers respect my ideas and opinions.					
8. I am an important member of my peer group.					

Evaluate your peer relations with an adult whom you respect. Describe ways you could improve your peer relationships.

_____

_____

_____

III. IMPROVING FAMILY RELATIONS

Teenagers frequently question their need to improve family relations. During adolescence, self-development and peer relations are of primary importance while family ties are often neglected or avoided. Improving family relationships is, however, a necessary and important part of growing to adulthood.

• RULES AROUND THE HOUSE

Listed below are ground rules for family unity. Hold a family meeting to discuss the importance of each statement. Add your own rules, if necessary.

1. Family members are aware and supportive of the needs of each individual.

2. Individual and group expectations are discussed and agreed upon.

3. Family chores are identified and met in a democratic manner.

4. The need for privacy should not inconvenience others.

5. New ideas are encouraged and acted upon.

6. Problems are discussed in an open, respectful manner.

7. Respect for one another's possessions is evident.

8. Having fun together is a family value.

9. _____

10. _____

• MEETING NEEDS

Write the name of a family member in the first box. Describe a goal or need possessed by this person in the second box. Tell how you could assist this person in meeting his/her need in the third box. Follow this procedure for each member of your family.

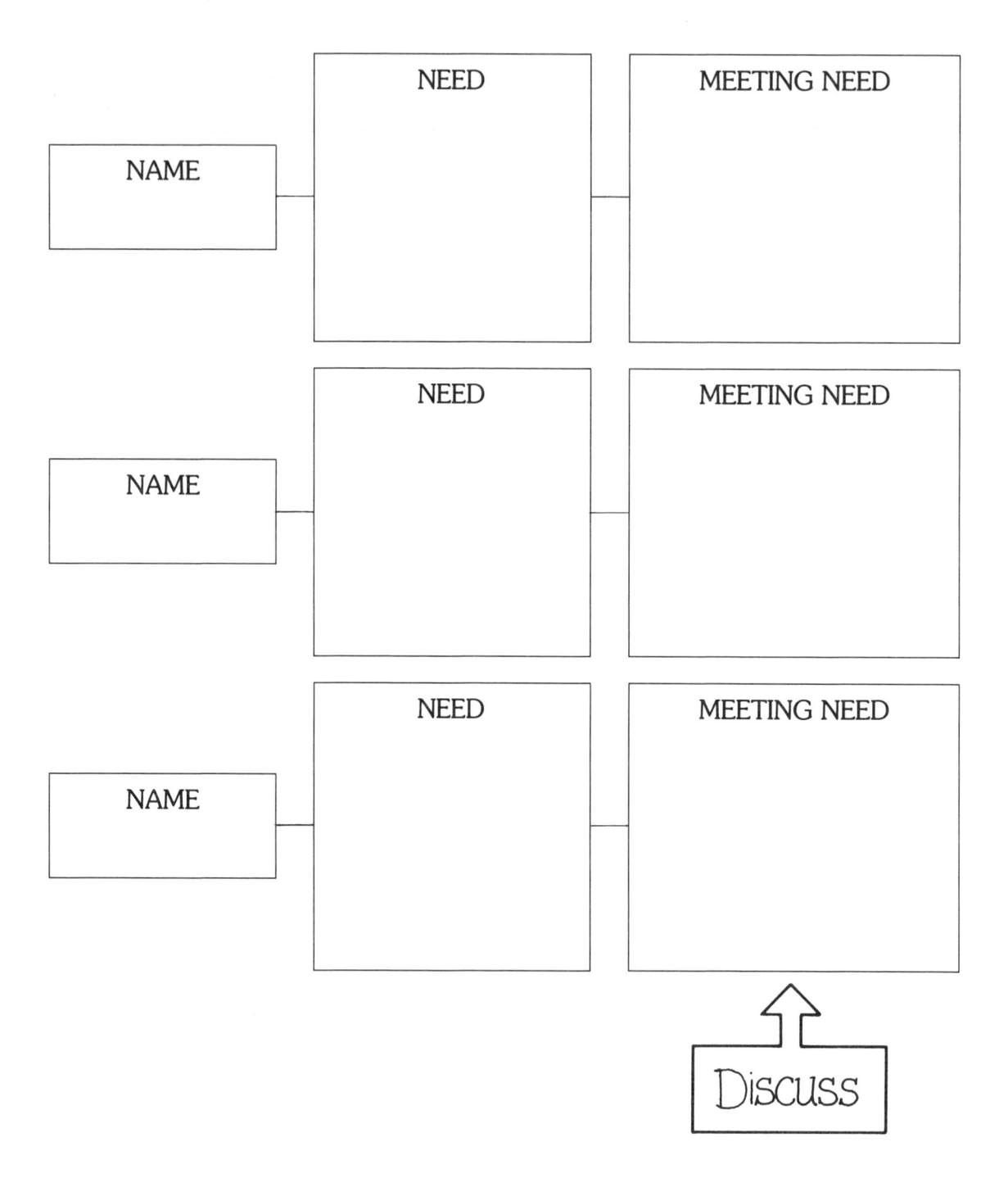

NAME	NEED	MEETING NEED
NAME	NEED	MEETING NEED
NAME	NEED	MEETING NEED

⇧ Discuss

• STATING EXPECTATIONS

Expectations often are unspoken and, therefore, unfulfilled. At a family meeting, state those things you expect of your family. Ask family members to state their expectations for you. Write these expectations in the spaces provided.

Discuss ⬇

I expect my family to
1. _____
_____
2. _____
_____
3. _____
_____

My family expects me to
1. _____
_____
2. _____
_____
3. _____
_____

• COMPLETING CHORES

List the family chores that you are expected to complete on a regular basis. Put the number in the box to indicate the following:

1. complete without being reminded.
2. complete with occasional reminding.
3. complete with frequent reminding.

Discuss ↓

☐ _____
_____

☐ _____
_____

☐ _____
_____

☐ _____
_____

☐ _____
_____

Did you have any choice in acquiring your chores? Are all the chores equally distributed among family members? May chores be exchanged among family members? Conduct a family meeting to answer these and other questions you might have.

34

• FINDING PRIVACY

Listed below are common times when teenagers desire privacy. At what time, however, does the need for privacy become an inconvenience for others? Complete each of the statements below. Discuss your responses with your classmates.

Discuss ⬇

1. My time on the *telephone* becomes an inconvenience to others when _____

2. My time in the *bathroom* becomes an inconvenience to others when _____

3. My time to *myself* becomes an inconvenience to others when _____

4. My time with *my friends* becomes an inconvenience to others when _____

5. My time with _____ becomes an inconvenience to others when _____

• SHARING IDEAS

It is usually beneficial to have help in making decisions, solving problems and implementing new ideas. At a meeting, discuss the hopes and goals of your family. Determine a way of making one new idea a concrete reality.

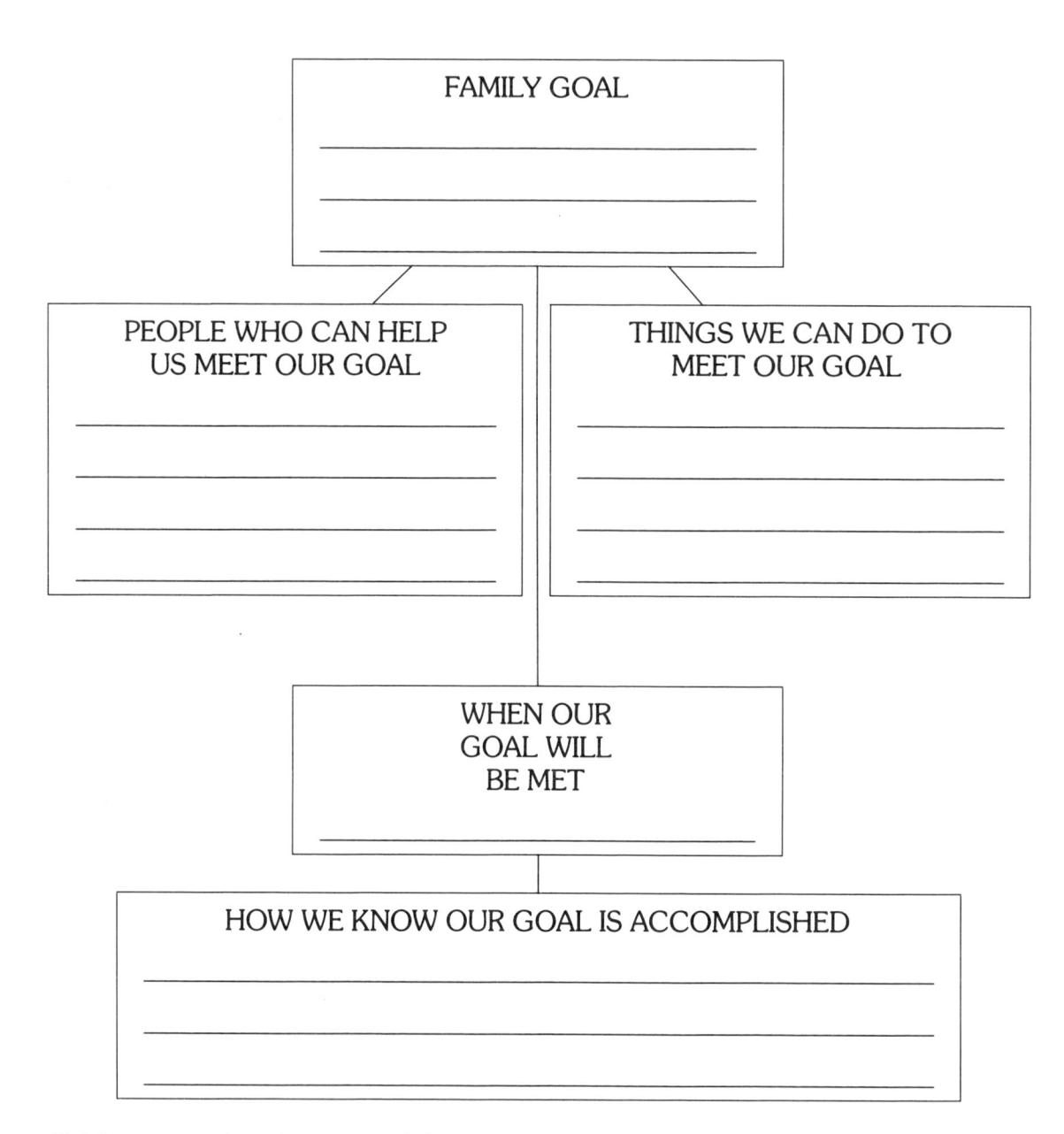

```
                    ┌─────────────────────────┐
                    │      FAMILY GOAL        │
                    │   _____   │
                    │   _____   │
                    │   _____   │
                    └─────────────────────────┘
                     /            |           \
┌──────────────────────────┐       ┌──────────────────────────┐
│  PEOPLE WHO CAN HELP     │       │  THINGS WE CAN DO TO     │
│     US MEET OUR GOAL     │       │     MEET OUR GOAL        │
│  _____   │       │  _____   │
│  _____   │       │  _____   │
│  _____   │       │  _____   │
│  _____   │       │  _____   │
└──────────────────────────┘       └──────────────────────────┘
                              |
                    ┌─────────────────┐
                    │   WHEN OUR      │
                    │   GOAL WILL     │
                    │    BE MET       │
                    │  _____  │
                    └─────────────────┘
                              |
        ┌────────────────────────────────────────────┐
        │  HOW WE KNOW OUR GOAL IS ACCOMPLISHED      │
        │  _____  │
        │  _____  │
        │  _____  │
        └────────────────────────────────────────────┘
```

Celebrate together the accomplishment of having met this group goal.

• DISCUSSING PROBLEMS

It is possible to respect other people's opinions without agreeing with each position. State your opinion on each of the topics listed below. State your parents' opinions on these same issues.

TOPIC	MY OPINION	MY PARENTS' OPINION
DATING		
ALLOWANCE		
CURFEW		

Discuss with your parents their opinions on these topics. Circle the answer that best completes the statement below.

My interpretation of my parents' opinions is

    very accurate

    somewhat accurate

    somewhat inaccurate

    very inaccurate

Discuss

• RESPECTING POSSESSIONS

List those things you own and value as an individual. List those things you own and value as a family.

THINGS I OWN & VALUE	THINGS MY FAMILY OWNS & VALUES

Put a check (✓) in front of those possessions that could be better respected by yourself and your family.

Conduct a meeting to discuss how personal and group possessions might be better respected by all family members.

• CELEBRATING TOGETHER

Write the names of family members in the space below. Describe what each person does for relaxation and enjoyment.

NAME   RELAXATION ACTIVITIES

_____   _____

_____   _____

_____   _____

_____   _____

_____   _____

_____   _____

Examine the various relaxation activities of each family member.

Conduct a family meeting to determine three quality activities that can be enjoyed by the entire family. State these activities below. Commit to participating in at least one activity on a regular basis.

_____

_____

_____

• ADDING TO FAMILY UNITY

Meet as a group to discuss how family unity is encouraged by individual attitudes and actions. Write those factors which contribute to family unity on strips of paper. Cut out the strips. Tape or staple these strips together to make a family unity chain. Display the chain in a prominent place in your home.

Share some of the factors which contribute to family unity in the space below.

FAMILY UNITY IS ENCOURAGED BY:

_____
_____
_____
_____
_____
_____
_____
_____
_____
_____
_____

⬆
| Discuss |

Family unity is encouraged by

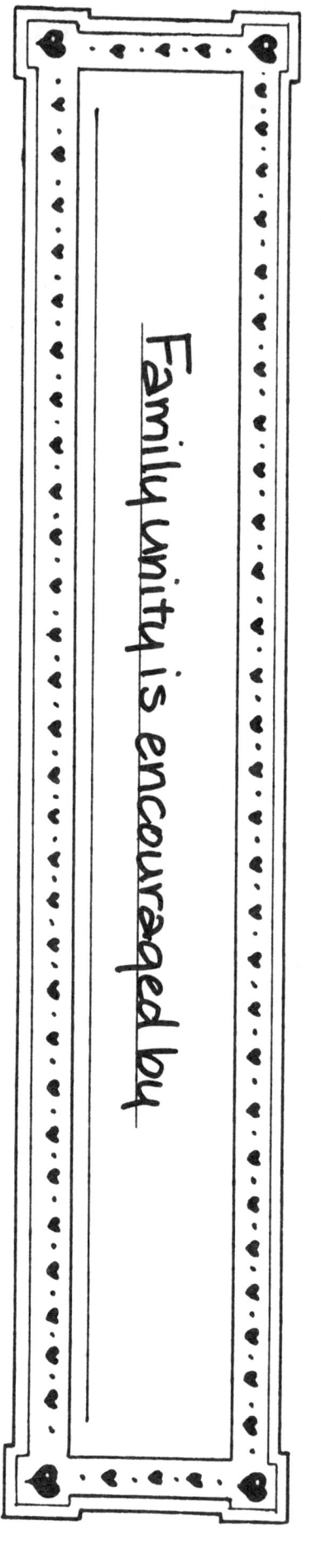

40

• SHOWING APPRECIATION

Suggest ways to express your appreciation for the members of your family in the space provided.

Discuss ⬇

I could show that I appreciate

_____ by _____

_____ by _____

_____ by _____

_____ by _____

_____ by _____

_____ by _____

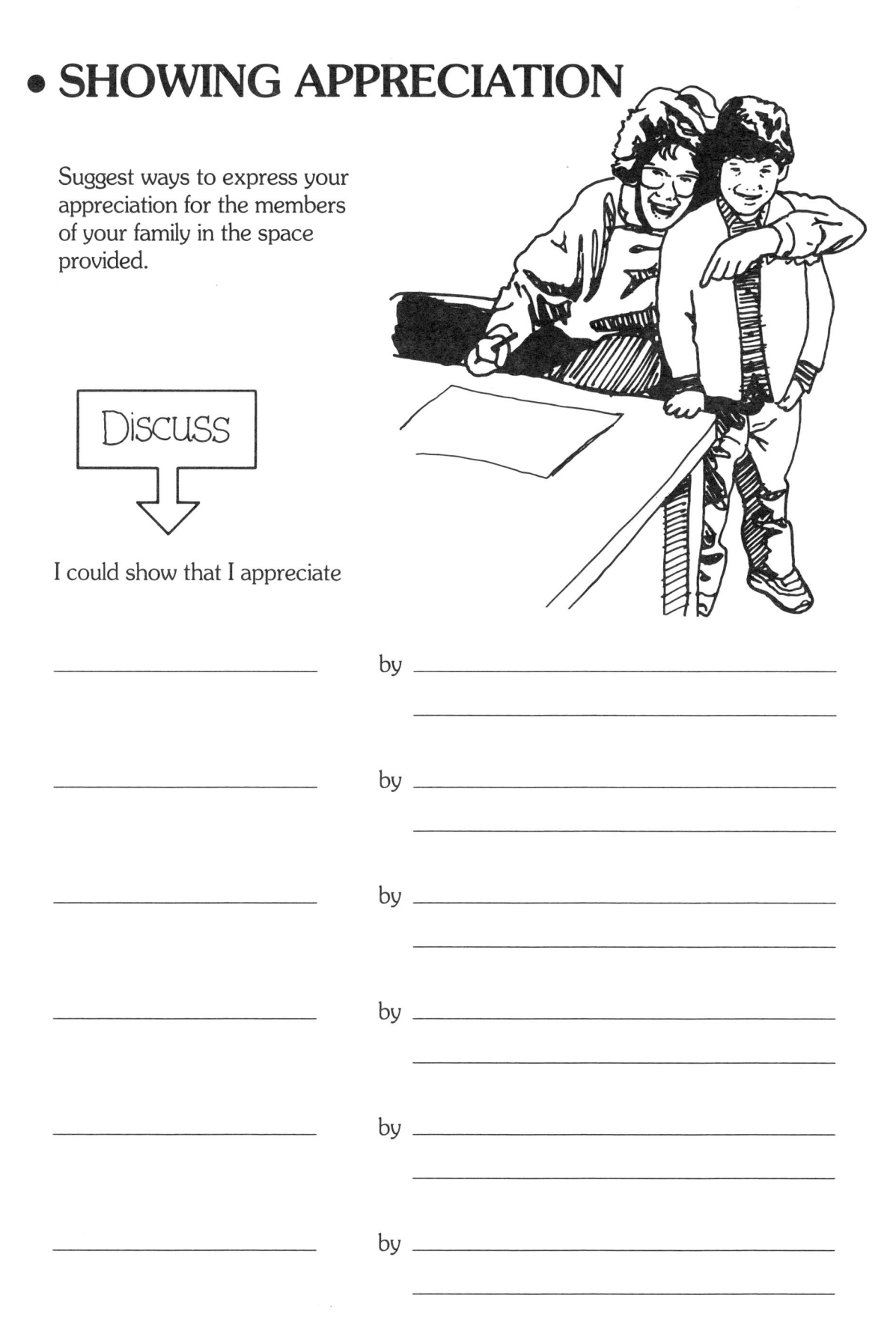

Put a star (*) before the name of one family member. Show this person that you appreciate him/her as a family member within a 24-hour period. Choose another family member and show this person your appreciation. Continue this procedure until you have shown appreciation for each member of your family.

• GROWING AS A FAMILY

Conduct a family meeting to complete the following statements.

1. Three positive words to describe our family are
   _____
   _____
   _____

2. A goal we have as a family is
   _____
   _____

3. Those things we like best about our family are _____
   _____
   _____
   _____

4. Three possessions we value as a family are
   _____
   _____
   _____

5. We relax and enjoy ourselves as a family by
   _____
   _____
   _____
   _____
   _____
   _____
   _____

IV. IMPROVING ADULT RELATIONS

Your family and friends have a strong influence on the attitudes and values that you acquire and the behaviors that you develop during adolescence. There are many other factors, however, that influence and affect your transition to adulthood.

• ADULT INFLUENCES

Listed below are adults who most likely affect your life in a significant way. Check (✓) the degree to which each person influences your life.

Degree to which the following people influence my life:

	Strongly	Somewhat	Not at all
1. parents	☐	☐	☐
2. grandparents and older people	☐	☐	☐
3. teachers	☐	☐	☐
4. employers	☐	☐	☐
5. employees	☐	☐	☐
6. dentists/doctors	☐	☐	☐
7. vocal groups	☐	☐	☐
8. TV/movie stars	☐	☐	☐
9. political figures	☐	☐	☐
10. _____	☐	☐	☐

• RELATING TO MY PARENTS

The attitudes, values and behaviors of your parents have a profound influence on your life as a child, adolescent and adult. Write your answers to the following statements. Discuss your thoughts and feelings with your mother and father.

My mom strongly influences my life by

_____
_____
_____

My dad strongly influences my life by

_____
_____
_____

I could improve my relationship with my parents by

_____
_____
_____

My parents could improve their relationship with me by

_____
_____
_____

Discuss

44

• RELATING TO OLDER PEOPLE

Check (√) the most appropriate response to each statement.

Tell about the positive influence of older people in your life.

DISCUSS ⬇

OLDER PEOPLE	Usually	Sometimes	Seldom
1. are hard of hearing.			
2. are impatient with younger people.			
3. are forgetful.			
4. are a burden to society.			
5. know more than younger people.			
6. talk about the past.			
7. have too much time on their hands.			
8. are hazards on the highway.			
9.			
10.			

Discuss how the biases stated above can influence your opinions as an adolescent.

An older person who is a strong, positive influence in my life is

_____

This person is important to me because _____

_____

_____

One of the best times I ever had with this person was _____

_____

_____

```
┌─────────────────────────────────┐
│                                 │
│                                 │
│                                 │
│                                 │
│         Paste a photo of this   │
│         special person here.    │
│                                 │
│                                 │
│                                 │
│                                 │
└─────────────────────────────────┘
```

I could show this person my respect and love by _____

_____

_____

Note: You may want to let this special person know that he/she is an important influence in your life.

• RELATING TO TEACHERS

You spend more than 1000 hours a year with your teachers. Your teachers can be a strong influence in your life. Check (✓) the appropriate response to each statement.

My teachers	STRONGLY	SOMETIMES	SELDOM
1. provide classrooms that are comfortable, attractive and conducive to learning.			
2. provide learning activities that are worthwhile and interesting.			
3. involve me in the planning of lessons and projects.			
4. offer special assistance when I am in need of help.			
5. are concerned about my emotional and social development.			
6. communicate effectively with me and other students.			
7. genuinely respect and care about me.			
8. genuinely enjoy their work.			

A teacher who I highly respect is _____

This person is a strong, positive influence in my life because _____

_____

_____

Note: You may want to tell this person that you respect and appreciate him/her.

• RELATING TO EMPLOYERS

Employers can play an important role in your life. There may be positive and negative aspects to being employed as a teenager. Describe and discuss the advantages and disadvantages of your job (or the job you hope to have in the near future).

JOB DESCRIPTION	ADVANTAGES	DISADVANTAGES

Describe the job you hope to have as an adult. Tell about the advantages and disadvantages of this work.

_____
_____
_____
_____
_____
_____
_____

• RELATING TO EMPLOYEES

It is important to foster good relations with those people who provide various services on a day-to-day basis. Tell how you would improve the situations described below.

SITUATION	SOLUTION
You and a friend receive the wrong sandwiches. The waitress insists that your order is correct.	
You return a recently purchased hand tool that is defective. You are unable to find the sales slip and the clerk tells you that your money will not be refunded.	

Describe a recent problem you had while relating to an employee.
Describe your solution to this problem.

SITUATION	SOLUTION

• RELATING TO DOCTORS

Yearly medical checkups are especially important during your teenage years while your body is going through many changes. Check (✓) the box when you have learned the name, location and type of services provided by the following:

☐ *Family doctor.* You will either continue seeing your pediatrician or begin seeing a family doctor.

☐ *Health maintenance organization.* Check with your parents to see if you belong to a health insurance group.

☐ *Local health clinic.* Check with the school nurse or consult the Yellow Pages under clinics, health services or medical services.

☐ *Free clinic.* Check with the school nurse or consult the Yellow Pages under clinics.

Name three things you are doing or could do to take greater responsibility for your health and welfare.

_____
_____
_____
_____
_____
_____
_____
_____
_____
_____
_____

• INFLUENCE OF MEDIA

Music, movie and television stars can have a profound influence on your attitudes and values. Tell what you admire about the following people.

My favorite singer or vocal group is _____

because _____

_____

_____

My favorite movie star is _____ because

_____

_____

_____

My favorite television star is _____ because

_____

_____

_____

Describe and discuss what your choices and comments tell you about your attitudes and values as a person.

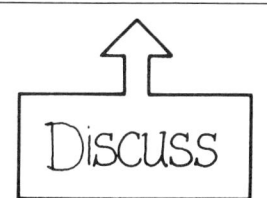

_____

_____

_____

Discuss

• INFLUENCE OF COMMERCIALS

Commercials are meant to influence your opinions regarding consumer goods. Paste magazine advertisements in the space provided. Write what each is attempting to emphasize. Discuss your ideas and opinions with your classmates.

• POLITICAL INFLUENCE

Public figures can affect your attitudes and behaviors in positive and negative ways.

Name a local leader whom you admire.

_____

Tell why you respect this person.

_____
_____
_____

Name a national leader whom you admire. _____

Tell why you respect this person.

_____
_____
_____

Name a world leader whom you admire. _____

Tell why you respect this person.

_____
_____
_____

If you could have a private appointment with one of these people, whom would you meet? _____

What would you talk about? _____

_____
_____

• EVALUATION

The purpose of the activities in this book is intended to help you better understand yourself, as well as improve your relations with family, friends and adults who influence your life.

I. UNDERSTANDING MYSELF

Put an X on the continuum that best describes your personality traits.

EXTROVERT _____ INTROVERT
INTUITIVE _____ SENSATE
THINKER   _____ FEELER
JUDGER   _____ PERCEIVER

II. IMPROVING PEER RELATIONS

Check (✓) the box that best describes your position at this time.

	Usually	Sometimes	Seldom
a. I know what my friends like and dislike.			
b. I am aware of the needs of my friends.			
c. I recognize and appreciate the uniqueness of my close friends.			
d. I keep peer relations free from expectations.			
e. I communicate in an honest way with my friends.			
f. I encourage my friends to develop other quality friendships.			

III. IMPROVING FAMILY RELATIONS

Check (✓) the box that best describes your opinions at this time.

Members of my family	Usually	Sometimes	Seldom
a. recognize and support each other's needs.			
b. discuss and agree upon individual and group expectations.			
d. recognize the need for privacy without inconveniencing one another.			
e. encourage and act upon new ideas.			
f. discuss problems in an open, respectful manner.			
g. respect each other's possessions.			
h. enjoy each other and have fun together.			

I communicate with my family
- ☐ very easily.
- ☐ somewhat easily.
- ☐ with some difficulty.
- ☐ with much difficulty.

One thing my family loves to do together is
_____
_____

I am proud of my family because
_____
_____

IV. IMPROVING ADULT RELATIONS

Use the following scale to describe your relationship with each of the adults in your life.

1 = excellent

2 = very good

3 = good

4 = poor

5 = very poor

_____ parents

_____ older people

_____ teachers

_____ employers

_____ employees

_____ doctors

Describe how you might improve your relationship with any people receiving a rank of 4 or 5.

_____

_____

_____

An adult whom I respect and admire is _____

because _____

_____

I communicate with people other than my family and friends

☐ very easily.
☐ somewhat easily.
☐ with some difficulty.
☐ with much difficulty.

BIBLIOGRAPHY
STUDENT RESOURCES

Books on growth and development can provide teenagers with answers to questions that they may not know how to ask. Books can provide the impetus for young people to reveal their own thoughts and feelings, as well as provide the framework for adult-child discussions on sensitive topics.

Before introducing a book to a student, it is very important that the teacher or parent first read the book. Familiarity with the book will assist the adult in answering questions a young person may have. It will also allow the adult to determine if a book's content is consistent with one's own belief in and approach to topics related to adolescent development.

Blume, Judy. *What Kids Wish They Could Tell You.* New York: Pocket Books, 1986.
   Shares the deepest concerns of teenagers and offers information as well as suggestions for happier, healthier teenage years.

McCoy, Kathy and Charles Ebbelsman. *Growing and Changing.* New York: Putnam Publishing Group, 1986.
   Addresses pressing questions and provides informed answers that make puberty easier to understand and accept.

Shaw, Diana. *Make the Most of a Good Thing: You.* JoyStreet Books. Boston: Little Brown and Co., 1986.
   Explores such problems as weight, exercise, getting along with parents and depression. Intended to help you take charge of your life.

Weston, Carol. *Girltalk.* New York: Barnes and Noble Books, 1985.
   Explores many problems teenagers face, from building solid friendships to coping with death.

Yothers, Tina and Roberta Plutsik. *Being Your Best: Tina Yothers' Guide for Girls.* New York: Pocket Books, 1987.
   Tina Yothers, of NBC's *Family Ties,* shares ways to be at your best in spite of the many problems teenagers face today.

ADULT RESOURCES

Bingham, Mindy, Judy Edmondson, Sandy Stryler. *Challenges*. Santa Barbara, California: Advocacy Press, 1984.
A young man understands himself, his feelings and his relationships. A guide to realistically planning for the future.

Bingham, Mindy, Judy Edmondson, Sandy Stryler. *Choices*. Santa Barbara, California: Advocacy Press, 1983.

Elkind, David. *The Hurried Child*. Menlo Park, California: Addison-Wesley Publications, 1981.
A look at young people in stressful circumstances. Offers suggestions to help improve these situations.

Elkind, David. *All Grown Up and No Place to Go*. Menlo Park, California: Addison-Wesley Publishing Co., 1984.
Parents are given the tools to help teenagers cope with the problems resulting from the social pressures of modern life.

Johnson, David W. *Reaching Out*. Englewood Cliffs, New Jersey: Prentice-Hall, Inc., 1972.
Suggests skills involved in initiating new friendships and maintaining present relationships.

Keirsey, David and Marilyn Bates. *Please Understand Me*. Del Mar, California: Promtheus Nemesis Books, 1978.
People are different from each other and these differences are good. The Jung-Meyers concept of mind type used and explained in vocabulary understandable to a general audience.

Kroll, Lillian and Joanne Ardolf. *Valuable You*. St. Cloud, Minnesota: Media and Materials, 1972.
A collection of meaningful activities designed to promote community among teenagers and important people in their lives.